D0495194

LONDON BOROUGH
THE QUEEN'S
C. E. SCHOOL
KEW
RICHMOND UPON THAMES

Look around you
Countryside

Ruth Thomson
Photography by Chris Fairclough

WAYLAND

First published in 2007 by Wayland

Copyright © Wayland 2007

Wayland
338 Euston Road
London NW1 3BH

Wayland Australia
Hachette Children's Books
Level 17/207 Kent Street
Sydney, NSW 2000

All rights reserved.

Editor: Victoria Brooker
Designer: Elaine Wilkinson
Design concept: Paul Cherrill

The author and publisher would like to thank: Forde Abbey; Polly Davies; Leigh-Anne Bennett; Adam Brona; John Primmer; Lyn Colenutt;Patrick Ward/Corbis for the picture page 14 (top) and Michael Nicholson/Corbis for the picture page 15 (bottom right)

British Library Cataloguing in Publicaton Data

Thomson, Ruth
In the countryside. – (Look around you)
    1. Rural geography – Juvenile literature 2. Country life –
    Juvenile literature 3. Human ecology – Juvenile literature
    I. Title
    910.9'1734

ISBN 978 0 7502 5147 1

Printed in China

Wayland is a division of Hachette Children's Books.

Contents

Words in **bold** can be found in the glossary.

Countryside everywhere

In Britain, there are many different types of countryside. In parts of the north and west there are mountains, deep valleys, lakes and moorland.

There are low, rolling hills in the south and flat, **fertile** land in the east.

▶ The highest mountains are in Scotland. Nothing grows on their rocky peaks.

▼ Moorlands are bleak, windy, rainy areas on high ground. Plants grow close to the ground in the thin, damp soil.

◀ More than three-quarters of the land in Britain is used for growing crops or grazing animals.

◀ In a few areas, there are **deciduous** woodlands. The most common woodland tree is the oak.

◀ Oak leaves and acorns

▶ Rivers run through the countryside. They always flow towards the sea.

Countryside features

Farming has helped to shape the countryside. Farmers have divided land into fields with hedges, walls or fences between them.

Narrow footpaths and wider **bridle paths** criss-cross the countryside. These are used by walkers, cyclists and horse riders.

▲ Strong, **drystone** walls keep sheep or cattle in or out.

▼ Hedges and trees act as **windbreaks**, as well as dividing fields.

▶ Walkers use footpaths. They cross from field to field over stiles or through gates.

 Stile

LOOK CLOSER!

There are farms all over Britain. Livestock farms raise cattle or sheep. Arable farms grow crops, such as wheat and barley. Some grow fruit or vegetables.

Farm

A water meadow with cattle

A field of leeks

Find out what animals are kept and what crops are grown in your nearest area of countryside.

Things of interest

Pylons, wind farms, water towers, **aqueducts** and **viaducts** are striking man-made landmarks in many parts of the countryside.

Some of the most remote, dramatic and beautiful areas of mountains, moors, woods and marshes are protected national parks. People enjoy exploring the wild landscape and spotting wildlife.

▲ Wind turns the long blades of these wind turbines to make electricity.

▼ Rows of pylons support cables carrying electricity from a power station to homes.

▲ Some roads and railway lines cross valleys on viaducts. This arched brick railway viaduct is in Ribblehead, in Yorkshire.

◀ Walking and climbing in the Lake District in north-west England is popular throughout the year.

▶ Ponies roam wild in Dartmoor, a national park in the south-west of England.

Dartmoor 40mph Zone

40

DARTMOOR NATIONAL PARK

Animals on Road Take Moor Care

Homes

There is space in the countryside for most houses to have a garden and often a garage for a car.

Farmhouses and large country houses are often surrounded by farmland. Farm workers sometimes live in small cottages belonging to the landowner.

▲ Farmhouses have outbuildings for animals and for storing crops and machinery.

▼ Grand country houses often have magnificent flower gardens and walled vegetable gardens.

◀ Old houses were built with local materials - brick, stone, wood, cob (mud and straw) or flint. This house has been partly built with wood.

▶ This new house in Yorkshire is built from stone and has a slate roof.

LOOK CLOSER!

What are old houses in your area made from?

What are new homes made from?

Flint and brick house

11

 # Work

Farmers plant crops in fields and look after animals that graze on lowland **pastures** or **uplands**. Foresters tend **plantations** of pine trees grown mostly for timber.

People also work in kennels for cats and dogs, nurseries and riding schools – which all need plenty of space.

▲ This man has been cutting watercress, which grows in clear spring water.

▼ After ploughing, which breaks up the earth, farmers sow their fields with seeds.

There are pine plantations in Scotland and Wales. When trees are cut down, their branches are sawn off.

These stable girls feed, groom and exercise horses at a riding school.

LOOK CLOSER!

What country jobs can you think of?

SUTTON GREEN NURSERY

GREAT VALUE   TOP QUALITY
HOME GROWN BEDDING
PYO   SHRUBS & TREES
Fruit
In Season   OPEN EVERY DAY

Signs of the past

Wherever you look in the countryside, you can usually see some sign of the past, such as a ruined castle, a country house, a fort or standing stones.

Many modern roads follow the line of Roman roads across country. Canals built more than two hundred years ago often still exist.

▲ Romans settled in Britain almost 2,000 years ago. Ruins of their buildings, such as this fort, can still be seen.

▼ Stonehenge is a circle of huge standing stones near Salisbury, in Wiltshire. It was put up four thousand years ago, but no-one knows exactly why.

▼ In the Middle Ages, monks lived together in great **abbeys**.

▶ There are castles in most parts of Britain, usually now in ruins. This castle at Rochester was built by the Normans soon after 1066.

◀ Canals were built to carry goods. Most were abandoned once railways were built, but they are now used for fun.

Moving around

Country lanes are often narrow and winding, and have no pavements. Newer, straighter motorways and **dual carriageways** now cut across the countryside. These link towns and cities.

Country buses do not usually run very frequently. Most people who live in the country own cars.

▲ Some lanes are wide enough for only one car. They have passing places for cars coming from the opposite direction.

▼ Cars travel fast on motorways and dual carriageways.

▶ This bus takes passengers from villages to a market town.

LOOK CLOSER!

People enjoy all sorts of activities that they can do in the countryside. Can you think of any others?

Walking

Motorbike racing

Downhill mountain bike racing

Cycling and horse riding

Farm shops

Farm shops mainly sell produce grown or made by local people. Some is grown **organically**.

Small farms provide vegetables, fruit and eggs. Beekeepers supply honey and other people make jams and chutneys. Gardeners supply cut flowers, pot plants and seedlings.

▲ Gardener

WEST LEA FARM SHOP

◀ The shop manager lays out a different display of local fruit and vegetables every day.

LOOK CLOSER!

Can you name all the vegetables that this farm shop sells?

LOOK CLOSER!

Visit a farm shop and list what it sells. Find out what is locally produced and what comes from other parts of the country or from elsewhere in the world.

Cake

Cheese

Quiche

Jam

Chutney

Honey

Mapping the countryside

Look closely at the map. Notice how:

- the main **dual carriageway** is much straighter than the smaller country roads
- the village is near a river
- the footpath goes across the countryside, crossing big as well as small roads

▼ Country house

▲ River   ▼ Woodland

Town

Dual caarriageway

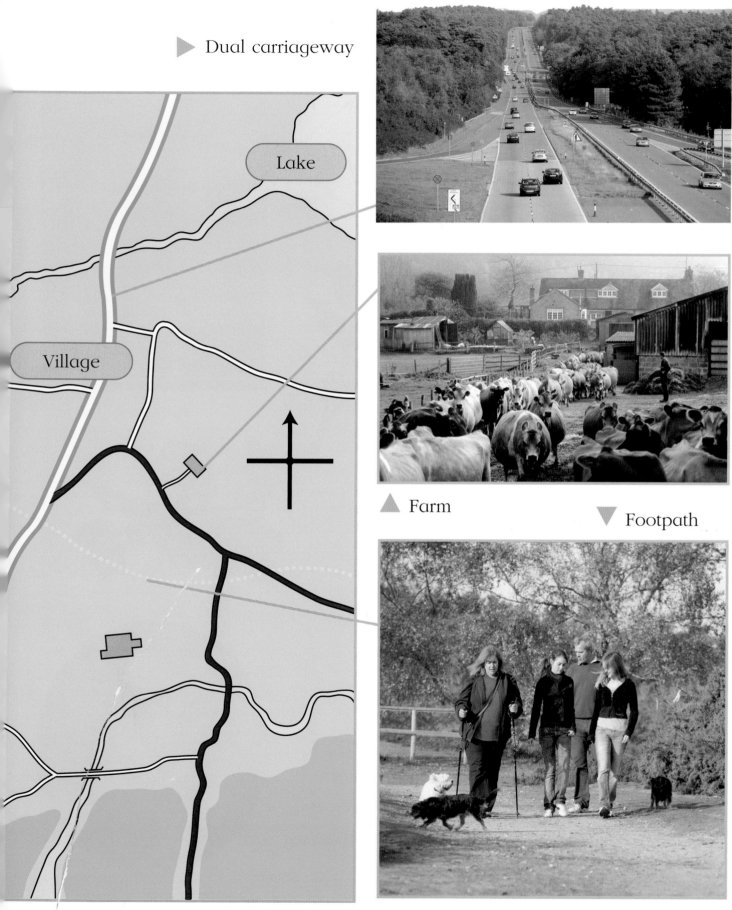

Dual carriageway

Lake

Village

Farm

Footpath

21

A walk in the countryside

Take a close look in woods, meadows and hedgerows when you go on a country walk. There is something new to see in every season.

Beech tree

Winter

In winter, **deciduous** trees are bare, but you can identify trees by their shape and their buds.

Holly

Evergreen plants, such as holly and ivy, keep their leaves in winter.

Ivy

Spring

In spring, as the days become warmer, the first flowers appear and trees come into blossom.

Snowdrops

Horse chestnut flowers

Summer

In summer, meadows and hedgerows are bright with wild flowers.

Dandelions

Poppies

Rosebay willowherb

Horse chestnut conkers

Autumn

In autumn, trees produce fruit. Some are nuts with hard shells. Berries are soft, juicy fruits.

Blackberries

Pine cones have winged seeds inside.

Rosehips